Jones,
meu amigo,
Obrigado pelo apoie,
tamo Junto!

Abraços

Proceed Progress

by Vitor de Souza

Acknowledgments and Inspirations

When I was a teenager in high school, I hated reading. It was extremely hard for me to pick up a book, let alone finish one. Towards my senior year, I was going through a hard time with my parents' divorce. I always knew my parents had issues but never thought they would one day get divorced. My dad, unfortunately, wasn't the biggest supporter of my mother when it came to her dreams and her way of thinking, and he gave us a hard time when something wasn't done his way. I always wanted to understand why he was stubborn and why couldn't he be more patient. My mother, couldn't accept the way my dad wanted things, therefore, they got divorced. I was blessed to gain the support from my girlfriend throughout these trying time. She was always there to console me throughout the arguments. Although her advice and comfort were always welcome, as they still are, I needed to find another way to deal with my emotions. That's when a co-worker at the time introduced me to the book *Don't Sweat the Small Stuff* by Richard Carlson.

I read a little of the book and immediately fell in love with the concept of it. That very same week, I went and purchased my own copy of it and read a little each day. I got to learn more about the things in life that stress us daily, and how we need to understand that we don't need to stress about everything. I loved how the chapters were short and easy to read; therefore, if I only wanted to read one chapter a day, I could. I read the entire book within a month. The book came into my life at a perfect time, as it helped me cope with the tough times I was going through. It was the first book I read entirely and felt passionate about it. From that moment forward, I started to put together my passions: I love helping people; I'm a caring and thoughtful person; and I'm intrigued to learn about why people act and feel certain ways. Therefore, I decided to major in psychology, as I felt that the major would provide not only a career but also a source of knowledge about the things that would happen in my life.

When I started college, I took many psych courses that confirmed my passion for psychology and self-development. I knew that by learning about the mind, not only would I be helping other people reach their full potential, but I would also be helping better myself at the same time. After studying and reading many different books about the subject, I started having my own ideas about how I could express my life in a way others could relate. Since the problem with my parents' divorce wasn't completely settled (largely because my dad struggled from time to time accepting it), I wanted him to feel what I did when I read the brilliant work by Richard Carlson. So, I started writing down my own thoughts. These thoughts were not only so my dad could one day read them and be proud, but it was a way I could share my experiences to help other people better themselves with the words I have written. The thoughts grow bigger and bigger, and I made it my goal that one day I would write a book. It's been a couple years since I started writing this book, and I honestly can't believe I'm publishing it now. I'm very excited to share my perspective of self-development with the world and touch as many peoples' heart as I can with it.

This book is dedicated to my family: My mother, Rosely, for always putting the needs of my brother and I first, and in her own way, being the best mom she could be; my father, Valdecir, for bringing me to live in the United States at the age of 12, giving me the opportunity to have a better future, thank you, dad; and for my brother, Caio, that even though we have our arguments and disagreements, like every other brother and sister have, you're the person I truly hope to make the proudest with this book; I love you all. I also dedicate this book to one of the most important people in my life, Emanuella, who has always been more than my partner, but a best friend, a woman who always stood by my side, through my best and my worst moments, because of the person she truly knows I am. To my closest friends, know that even if we stay apart for a long time, we are still connected in our hearts. You know who you are. Finally, I dedicate this book to you for deciding to take your time to read it. I hope you enjoy this book as much as I have enjoyed writing it. Thank you.

Contents

Introduction

We all seek many different things in life; some of us want to be successful in our careers, others want to travel the world, and others want to be rich and famous. While all these things are possible to reach if you set your mind to it, one thing I have learned is that everything in life is about *Proceeding and Progressing.*

Think about it, from the moment when we were kids and we did something our parents told us not to do, we might have done it a few more times because we were kids (it's just what kids do), and sometimes that specific something our parents were telling us not to do could bring harm to us somehow, such as when we touch something that is hot. Since we didn't listen the first time, now we're hurt, and although it's painful, we eventually learn to proceed with the situation by adapting to the injury and progress with our lives knowing not to do it again. Obviously, as kids, we didn't think of that, but when you stop to think about it, everything in life is about proceeding and progressing.

Throughout our lives, we will not only succeed in many things, but we will also fail. Many people may agree that we learn the most when we fail, but we also learn when we succeed. If you have landed a new job or a promotion, you will now learn about that new role, and so, you will be proceeding and progressing into it. Now, if you have gotten fired from your job, after going through the emotions of losing that job, you will go out to look for something else, and so, you have proceeded with your life and you are progressing into something new.

I have learned that for someone to be happy, they must learn that everything in life is about proceeding and progressing. We proceed with our lives when learning how to deal with downfalls, we progress into new roles and adventures, we adapt to challenges and changes, and so on. Sometimes life will throw you upside down, leaving you hopeless and unmotivated, but when you realize that everything can change and that when a door closes, two new ones open up, you will start to learn that every situation that life presents to you, you can move forward from it. This process is never-ending. You can become a millionaire of a huge company, and you will continue to proceed and progress in your life, by making decisions to innovate that business further or to invest your money elsewhere. We go through these never-ending steps of proceeding and progressing with everything in our lives, without even noticing it.

This book will consist of 50 small chapters that will highlight different situations and emotions we go through in our daily lives. In most cases, some chapters were written in relation to things I was going through in my life; therefore, I have used some of my personal experiences to paint a picture of a situation. One thing that I loved about the *Don't Sweat the Small Stuff* books, besides the great content that they had, were the size of the chapters. Since I wasn't a big reader at the time I read the first one, I loved how I could read a chapter a day if I wanted to. This book follows the same style. The chapters are small enough so that you are able to read a little each day, without needing to rush through it. *Proceed Progress* is about learning about yourself through my perspective. You will learn the importance of following your dreams and be a more positive person. You will learn the importance of adapting to changes. You will learn to *proceed and progress!*

1 : The speed of life

"If we would just slow down, happiness would catch up to us." – Richard Carlson

No better way to start this book than by talking about the speed of life. Life has many speeds. Sometimes the things we want come to us easy, and other times, we have to work really hard for it. Although most people would prefer to get everything they want as fast as possible, this is not always the best route.

We all have goals. Some of us have bigger goals than others. However, one thing we all have in common is that no matter how much you want to achieve these goals, life sometimes gets in the way. Sort of like being stuck in traffic; we are all trying to reach somewhere, but we get stuck in traffic that causes us to slow down. That doesn't mean you get out of your car and stop driving. You keep going. What I mean is that when the things we want to conquer are taking a little longer than what we wish for, maybe it is because it's not the right time for us to have it. All we see and think about is how unfair life is by not giving us what we want. We sit around complaining about things that are not going our way, wondering why can't we just get what we want, or be what we want. What most people don't consider is that where they're supposed to be, is the moment they are in right now. You can still get to exactly where you want to go and accomplish anything you want to, but sometimes you have to wait a bit. Sometimes you have to move at five mph to get to your dreams. We might not understand the real reason behind it, but learning to accept that we just are stuck in "traffic" helps us be patient for what's to come.

When we encounter "traffic," that is when we must take a step back and acknowledge what we have done so far, and analyze what's coming next. Don't get out of the driver's seat. This is still your life, and you're in control of it. So, when life slows you down, keep going, even if it's at five miles per hour . . . you can still get where you want. Even if you have to take a detour to get there. Keep going! You'll make it!

2: Time

When I was deciding where to place this chapter, I knew it was important to place it right after I spoke about the speed of life. Although I understand that sometimes it's better for us to move at five miles per hour to get where we want in life, I'm still one of the most anxious people I know.

I have a big problem with time. I'm always thinking that there's not enough time, for everything. If I am going to go out, before I actually go out, I'm always thinking that I'm late. I'm always guessing the time that I'm going to arrive at the set location, and I'm always estimating the amount of time I am going to be out for. There was a period in my life that I would constantly pick up my phone while driving to look at silly things. I did it because deep inside my head I felt that I was saving time by looking at these things while I was driving and not when I was at home. I have put my life and the people around me in danger, all because I thought that while driving was the best time to check my Instagram so that when I was home I could focus on the important things. I'm sharing this because I know that this is a big problem in the world. Think about how many people actually do this. Too many. We live in a world that runs on technology. Our phones vibrate and we want to check to see who wrote to us. We get a notification from social media, and we instantly want to check what it is. Considering these facts, there are probably many people that use their phone while driving, either to check silly things or simply because they believe something needs to be done right away. This is a huge problem in our world. Thankfully, I don't do that anymore because I noticed how dangerous it was. I learned to be more patient with things, and I learned that sometimes we have to wait to get where we want in life.

The point of this chapter is that most of us go through some kind of anxious moment against time. Either you just can't wait to buy a new car, or you're simply thinking that you're late for a party. At some point, we are faced with a situation that we are anxious about. Time is something we all battle with each and every day. We are either in a rush to get to work, or we are rushing to meet deadlines at work. Due to this, we might find ourselves trying to do things where we aren't supposed to, such as looking at our phones while driving to eliminate having to do that when we are at home, or even answering a work email when out with somebody special. We are always battling time, and we even endanger our lives and the lives of others doing so. We must find ways to take a step back and not let ourselves give in to these anxious moments. Sometimes when you take a step back, you will notice that what you might be stressing about is not even worth the headache. So, take a moment, breathe, find a way to get back to your normal state, and let your anxiety fly away.

3: Where are you going and where have you been

Have you ever stopped to think about where you are going and where you have been? Ever stop to see what you have accomplished in your life so far, or what you want to accomplish in the future? It is important to look back at the things we have done, and imagine the things we want to do in our lives, as it gives us meaning to keep going.

Part of proceeding and progressing is about knowing where you've been and where you want to go. It's very important to sometimes look back and see where you have been. Meaning, looking at the things you have accomplished or suffered in the past. I'm not saying for you to live in the past. Definitely not. I'm saying that sometimes in order for us to get where we are meant to be in our lives, it's important to recognize accomplishments and failures we have had along the way. Sometimes we are so busy with our daily lives that when we hit "traffic," we let the situation get us down. If we look back on our accomplishments, we remember the feelings we had in those moments, making us look forward to feeling that way again. When we look back at our failures, we remind ourselves that we have made it through something bad before, giving us a sense of hope to keep going through the barriers we might be facing now. Looking back on these moments can remind us that we have grown past those moments and we can do it again.

Along with looking back at our past, it's important to look at where we want to be in the future. Paint a picture of how you want it to be. Imagine all the little things you want to accomplish. That helps us process what we have to do to get there. Visualizing what we want to accomplish or where we want to be, helps us not forget our goals.

I've learned to keep my past at arm's reach when going into a situation where I can compare what I have gone through. As far as for my future, I'm a very excited person regarding where I want to be and what I want to accomplish. I'm always thinking ahead to what I want to accomplish in my career, such as writing this book or being a counselor. I'm always imagining how I will be as a husband or a father when that time comes around, as those are some of the things I look forward in my life. Thinking of my goals in the long term, helps me remember what I want my life to be, helping me focus on what I need to do to get there.

Sometimes life turns upside down, and we have to change our route; therefore, keeping in mind what we have gone through and where we want to be can help us maintain patience when taking that detour. Be optimistic, shoot high. The future is yours!

4: Be specific

I recently realized how important it is to be VERY specific. Specific about everything and anything. From the smallest thing ever to the most drastic situations. Simply just be specific! With time, days, hours, people, anything. You might think your point was understood, and then it really wasn't.

Not being specific can have some very negative consequences. For me, it cost my job. Or two jobs. March of 2016 will mark the time of my life where I learned to be specific. I was offered a big corporate job at one of the largest manufacturers of airplanes in the world. I decided to take this job because it was going to change my financial life drastically. So, I had to resign my position as a Microsoft Expert at Best Buy that I truly enjoyed. Before even considering this new position, my main concern was that I go to college. I knew that in that company, I had to be more flexible, but I wanted to make sure school was still something I could attend. Therefore, before my interview, I asked about the schedule and if they would be flexible with my classes, at least for the semester that had already started. I got the answer through an email that the company understands personal life and would be flexible. I made sure that during my interview, I brought up the classes again. I made sure they knew I was going to school and that I didn't want that to be a problem. The response from the hiring manager was that they would be flexible and that I shouldn't worry. When I received the call with the job offer, I made sure I asked one more time. The response again was that it would be okay. I got the job, and I was extremely happy for this opportunity to make decent money—all while still going to school—at a company I had admired for years.

So, the first day comes along. Everything is going smoothly. I got to introduce myself to the department where I was going to work in. I got to meet the entire facility and the numerous employees on the other departments. As the morning was almost done, I walked into my manager's office and asked if he had a minute to speak about my schedule. Once again, he tells me not to worry, and that we could speak about it after lunch. When I returned from lunch, my manager asked the times I needed for my classes. He wasn't very happy to find out that I had to leave early from work two days of the week. He was really upset that an employee that just got there couldn't be there when they needed. I explained that this was only for another month until that semester ended and that in the future I would pick classes at night. Long story short, I couldn't stay in that job. So, I was let go after six hours of work. I felt that the manager could have been more interested in the times I went to school prior to hiring me, instead of telling me I shouldn't worry about it because they are "flexible," but that's when I learned the importance of being specific.

The point of this story is that it doesn't matter how much you think somebody comprehends what you meant, it is ALWAYS better to be specific about everything. If I told them from the beginning I had classes, these days, at these specific times, I probably wouldn't have been hired. I probably wouldn't have left my other job as a Microsoft Expert at Best Buy. Turns out I lost two jobs that month.

So be specific, your message is not truly delivered unless you tell the other individual exactly what you mean. Sometimes you think your point was understood, and it truly wasn't. The moment I was fired from that job, I was hurt. I couldn't believe that it was simply because of a misunderstanding. I learned a valuable lesson to be more specific to others about our needs and desires. Furthermore, I also learned that I wasn't mean to be in that job, but that will we discuss in another chapter.

5: Always hope for the best

"We must accept finite disappointment but never lose infinite hope."
– Martin Luther King Jr.

Life will always have its negatives routes. Sometimes we might not understand why things such as losing a job after six hours happen to us. It is important to know that bad things can always happen, but we must always hope for the best.

What some of you don't know is that negative routes are only there to remind us to never forget our "meaning markers." Meaning markers as explained by Shawn Achor in the book *Before Happiness*, are the things that mean the most in your lives. The things that although you might not have it right now, they are what you want the most. For example, being successful in the workplace, being a great husband, or a great father, buying a home, or living overseas. When your life gets tough, it's only to remind you what you're doing it for.

Only to remind you that all of this will be worth it when you get to accomplish your "meaning markers." It is important to get past negativity fast and not let your stressors take over your life (Achor). Being pessimistic can cause you to miss out on great opportunities. So even when your life is going great, and you have everything you want at that moment, if something bad comes along, don't let it ruin your moment. Keep pushing forward.

When life gets hard, just know that it only does that to remind you of what it's all for. It's just testing your faith to keep going. Don't give up. That way, you can turn the page of negatively and get back to your meaning markers! Challenges will rise, mistakes will be made, and disappointments will happen, however, we must never lose our infinite hope to keep going.

6: Visualize success

"See yourself living in abundance and you will attract it. It works every time with every person." – Bob Proctor

Knowing your goals in life is something very important in the process of proceeding and progressing. However, visualizing success is as important as the process of knowing those goals.

So, what do I mean by that? Visualize your life when you have already accomplished your goals, think of how it can be, or how you wish it to be. Having that mentality helps your brains to never forget your goals, making them more possible for you. Again, this is different than the chapter about knowing where you're going in life. This is about visualizing your success past the moments that you have achieved your goals. See yourself past the moment of landing that job or passing that test. How do you feel about it? This not only can be applied to long-term goals, but also for short-term goals.

For example, if you are playing a very important basketball game, and you need to make that shot during the last seconds, visualize your success of making that shot and how good you will feel saving the team and winning that game. Or if you have a project due for your school or work, and maybe you're stressed about the amount of work that is demanded of you. Instead of focusing on how hard it can be, visualize yourself after you're done with it, and how rewarding it would be to get that good grade in your class or make your boss happy.

By visualizing success at all times, even in times of pressure, your brain stays focused on that goal, making it more possible for you. The same works if you wish to be successful in your career one day and live a stable life. Always remember to visualize your success, even if it still very far away, as that helps your brain remember the things that are important to you.

Don't get me wrong, there are many people in this world that imagine themselves being successful, rich, or famous, and they don't necessarily reach their goals. That's because visualizing your success doesn't mean that they will come to you. That just helps you stay positive so you can go after them. Meaning, you still have to practice to make that shot at the basketball game, or put in many hours of work to finish that project for your school or work. Nothing comes easy, but by visualizing how things can be when your goals are done, short-term or long-term goals, you find a purpose for going after them. In addition, visualizing your success helps you attract it, but that we will discuss that in the next chapter.

7: Aladdin

> "If you can dream it, you can do it."
> – Walt Disney

The same way that visualizing success can help you stay focused on your goals, wishing for the things we want in life helps us get where we want as well.

I'm sure most of us have watched the movie *Alladin*. We all loved the way that his wishes came true when he discovered the genie in the bottle. What if I told you that in order for you to get what you want, you have to be a little more like Aladdin? Sounds silly? But it's true! Think about, if you take out the genie of the story, all Aladdin did was wish for something. He wished for it so hard that he attracted it. And that's what most of us don't do in our lives. We forget to wish for things we want in order to attract them. We get so caught up in life's struggles that we sometimes forget to envision the things that we actually want. In the famous book and film *The Secret*, where many different people speak about the Law of Attraction, they explain how we have to wish for the things that we want, believe in them, in order to receive them. That's what Aladdin did. Well, he did have a genie that granted his wishes. But the moral of the story is that although he was a simple man, he had wishes, and he believed in them. And so, his wishes came true.

By the way, if you have never heard of *The Secret*, you should stop everything you are doing right now and go watch it or read it. It's basically everything we must learn to live by.

Anyways . . . be optimistic, wish for things, visualize your success, go after them, and believe you will get them. Believe it, and you shall receive it! What you think about, it's what you will bring to your life! It's the law of attraction. It worked for Aladdin, and it can definitely work for you!

8: Judge people

We grow up listening to our parents and adults telling us not to judge people. Telling us that is an ugly thing to do, and how you wouldn't like it if it was done to you. Truth is, we all judge people. We judge our family members' decisions, we judge our friends and the things they do, and we judge everybody with what we know about them. Although it's not cool to judge people to their faces, talk bad about them to others, or criticize people, I have learned that it's very important to judge people to help us see where we are in life.

Wait . . . I know what you are thinking, but hear me out. I started to notice that although we are taught not to judge people, we all do. We judge others around us as they judge us. We are constantly analyzing people's job status, income, relationships, the way they act, etc. Now that the internet is such a powerful tool for putting our daily lives out there, we are constantly judging the things people post about their lives. Either about how they post nonsense stuff, or how they pretend to have different lives on the web. The point is, we all are constantly judging many things that other people do, either online or in their actual lives. There's no denying that. But what if I told you that judging others can help shape your personality and remind you of the things that matter to you?

We do it without noticing it, but when we are judging the things our friends, family, or those around us are doing, we are reminding ourselves of the things that we value. We are reminding ourselves to go do what we like, either because a person has shown us what happens if we don't, or maybe because another person has done something similar and it gave us the inspiration to go after it. Judging people is a form of self-development we all do without knowing. It helps us to see what people around us are doing with their lives. It makes us see where we are standing in our lives. It helps us remind ourselves of our true values and goals. Now, don't take this the wrong way, because is not okay to go around telling other people bad things about others. That's not okay. It is also not okay to criticize people and point out their mistakes, as it doesn't encourage them to change, it only brings them down. You shouldn't compare yourself to others in a way that will make you feel bad for what you have either. Overanalyzing the life of another will only bring you down. The kind of judgment and comparison I'm talking about here is the kind that can help you better yourself.

Judging a person that is doing something you disagree with, helps you remember your values; also, judging those that are doing something right in their life such as the successful people you admire, helps you align your goals. The key to this chapter is to turn the judgment into an inspiration to do better. So, judge people to inspire you or to align your values, you'll be surprised by all the great things it can bring to you.

9: Self-portrait

Most people don't realize the importance of taking things more seriously. I have worked with some people in the past that just don't care one bit about the job that they are in. And sometimes when I ask them about it, the answer most of the time is that they don't like their job, or because this is not their career, or because they simply just don't care. It is so important to take most things seriously, especially a job.

I always have done my best at every job I've had. Even when I worked at the café at a Target store which was probably the worst job I ever had (or will ever have). When I relocated to Melbourne, Florida, and moved away from my mother's home (for the first time), I had to get the first job I could find, so I ended up at Target. I hated working there. I would have to prep pizzas and pastas, bake cookies and pretzels, mop the floor, and wash dishes. I felt so low. I knew I had the potential for so much more. Although I hated working at Target, I always did my best. Sure, I had my bad days where I didn't want to do anything, especially working there. However, I still did my best for the most part. Many customers left happy after I helped them, and many of those customers sometimes wrote to the store manager about my service. I always had a smile on my face and tried to do everything as well as I could, not only for the customers but for my co-workers.

Some people I worked with in the past simply didn't care. They didn't understand how valuable it is to take things more seriously. The most important reason to always do the best you can in all situations and at every place you go to, such as a job, is simply because of the image you provide of yourself. When you leave that job that you hate, you can leave with your head up high. Simply because what will be remembered of you is the portrait you have left behind. I'm not saying that the Manager from Target remembers me now after years, but the image I gave of myself was left to everybody, to my co-workers, my customers, and even for myself. I guarantee you, at least one person, will remember your self-portrait. You never know when you might encounter a person in your life again. You don't want to be remembered as the lazy one that did a horrible job simply because you hated working at that certain place. You want to be remembered for the inspiration you gave to others to do their very best.

As you grow older, you will be remembered by at least one person from every place you been through, either from a job, a sports team, or from your school. You want to portray a nice image of yourself. You will feel better leaving your mark behind from every place you had been, even if you do not intend to stay there the rest of your life. You never know when you will need that person or that job. So, do your best, at everything you do, you're only helping yourself by doing so.

10: Find meaning in people and things.

One day, I was at a bar with a friend of mine, we were talking about some decisions that he was thinking about making soon. A guy that was sitting next to us by himself overheard our conversation and started explaining that in life everything has a meaning. He started out by mentioning that everything in this world has meaning: people, movies, and even objects in a room.

His ideas sounded a bit crazy to me at first, especially coming out from a guy sitting at a bar that I watched imbibe a couple of beers earlier. But then he started explaining that a room with different tones of lights, gives different atmospheres, such as why a bar is dimmer than a library. The way chairs are placed in a room is what will make the room more engaging for conversations or not. OK, this is not a design course on how rooms should be set up differently, this is about how literally everything in life has a meaning.

The guy in the bar took the conversation to a higher level, explaining how every person and animal on this earth is equal and we all have a meaning as well. He mentioned that different animals feed other animals in order to feed us humans. The reason the guy interfered with the conversation I was having with my friend, was to help my friend set meaning to the decision he was deciding upon and see which had a greater meaning to him. We left the bar that night, and from that day forward I started to analyze his theory with everything I saw. I'm not sure if that moment I shared with my friend at the bar had an impact on him, but for me, it changed my life. I started looking at how everything provides meaning. I started to look at animals on the street differently, by thinking what can they be possibly thinking about. I started to understand why things were placed a certain way or why things happened a certain way in our lives. I started to give meaning to people and things.

The point of this weird chapter is that everything and person in this world are equal and provides meaning. I find meaning in everything I do and see. I watch a movie, and I find important moments that highlight a character. I listen to many different types of music and try to find meaning in most of the lyrics, from a beautiful Coldplay song, or to a rap song by Drake. Sometimes that movie or that song can have a simple scene or a simple line that brings meaning to me, other times, the entire movie or song has a huge meaning. The point of it all is that I seek meaning in everything: music, movies, an environment, people, etc.

Finding meaning in everything gives us a sense of feeling alive. Keeps us connected to the world. It's important to be connected with our introspections, which is when we look inward to examine our thoughts, feelings, and motives, that way we can identify the things that matters to us. But it is equally important to know that everybody else has their own introspection, and everything else has a meaning in their lives. Finding meaning also helps us make decision better, by deciding what options play a bigger part in our lives.

So, the next time you are going through something, think about how it might have a meaning, or when you come across an important decision that you need to make, look within and find which has greater meaning to you. We go about our lives sometimes forgetting to appreciate the smallest things, but even the smallest thing can sometimes have a big meaning. Take a moment to analyze the things that have a big meaning to you. Analyze a special song, or a movie scene, and give it meaning that you can carry in your life. Sometimes I listen to a song, or watch a movie, and find something meaningful on it, that I can carry throughout my life. Analyze the people that come into your life and what they bring to you. Analyze situations you are in, good and bad ones, and see what they are offering you. Many things in life provide meaning. Start looking for them.

11: Give feedback where feedback is due

I believe that feedback is one of the most important things we all need to live a better life. Although we prefer receiving positive feedback, negative feedback is equally important when it comes to self-development.

I'm a person that loves feedback. If I'm doing an excellent job at work, I appreciate it so much when a leader comes up to me and tells me I'm doing good. I like it more when the person goes into detail about what I did well. It makes me feel good, and it motivates me to keep it up. I also like to receive negative feedback. However, it must be informative and not in a way that will put me down. Negative feedback helps me realize what I'm doing wrong and what I can fix.

But why can't we all be like that for everything? Not only for work but in life itself. Meaning: why don't we all tell our significant other at all times when they are being a great friend. Or when they have made you happy. Or even when you think they could have done something better for you or for themselves. Why do we hesitate in telling the truth? Is it because we feel afraid it might hurt them, or is it because we just don't want to have that kind of conversation? It's hard, it really is. If we could do that, we would all be better with each other. But instead most of the times we let it go thinking it will go away, but sometimes it just makes it worst. So why can't we give feedback, where feedback is due?

For the most part, I do an excellent job telling others that they have done a good job at work, or telling my girlfriend how important it was for her to support me with something, but I do struggle giving negative feedback sometimes, don't you? We struggle so much by contemplating how the person receiving the feedback is going to act or what that person will say, that we become afraid of doing so. I know! Trust me, I'm writing about this because I go through the same thing. It's extremely difficult to know when to give that feedback. However, sometimes we hold so much in, that we end up giving our feedback in the form of letting everything out, almost as if we hate that person, and that's not always the case. So why can the negative feedback be easier to give? If you think about it, both forms of feedback are implied to tell a person something they did right or wrong, so they can better themselves, either by continuing to act that way or changing their ways, so we shouldn't be afraid of helping them.

Feedback is a very important form of self-development. The more feedback people receive, the more information they will have to better themselves. So, give feedback, good and bad. Don't be afraid of what you have to say. If you respectfully present your points, the receiver will eventually understand where you're coming from. Everything can be a resource for a better life, even feedback.

12: Don't be afraid

Most people suffer from this one simple issue: Being afraid. We are simply afraid of many things in our lives, such as pursuing our dreams, not giving up when we get knocked down, or even something as simple as giving feedback as explained in the previous chapter. In order for us to proceed into a happier life, we have to learn not to be afraid. Don't be afraid of trying new things. Don't be afraid of change. Don't be afraid to start over. Don't be afraid to do anything.

Being afraid is something we are taught by society, friends, and even through our families. We see a sad movie and we are afraid that something similar can happen to us. We see our friends and family going through hard times, and we are afraid of going through the same things. Now, the most classical form of being afraid is taught by the people around us. When we want to do something for ourselves, and we ask the opinions of others, they discourage us from going after it, simply because they think they can't accomplish something themselves.

As I mentioned in a previous chapter, I try to make meaning of most things in my life. From a situation in real life to a movie scene. In the movie *Pursuit of Happyness*, based on the autobiography of entrepreneur

Chris Gardner, there is a scene that gives a perfect example of how people that we love can sometimes discourage us. When Chris is playing basketball with his son Christopher Jr., he tells his son that he shouldn't be playing basketball every day, as he probably will be only as good as his father was. Chris discourages his son from following a passion simply because he wasn't good himself. Have you ever been in a similar situation? Maybe with a parent or even a close friend? You tell them your big idea, and they sound discouraging simply because they think that what you want to accomplish is too hard, so they give you answers based on how they feel about the situation. In most cases, that creates fear in us that prevent us from pursuing what we want. This is because the people we care about the most think it's not worth it, or that is too hard.

We are afraid of many things in our lives. We are afraid of pursuing our dreams, we are afraid of speaking up in times we need to give feedback, we are afraid of trying new things, etc. Sometimes this fear is brought upon us by our peers, making us more unmotivated for pursuing what we want. We must learn to let go of that fear. Follow your heart and let go of what scares you, don't always believe in things people say, be spontaneous, take chances, try new things, meet new people, go to new places, and most importantly don't be afraid of living!

13: Everything happens for a reason

"Eventually all things fall into place. Until then, laugh at the confusion, live for the moments, and know everything happens for a reason."
– Albert Schweitzer

I know you heard that before . . . but have you ever been in a position where you truly see everything happening and then maybe at the time you don't understand it, but then as things fall into place, you start to really notice how everything really does happen for a reason?

A little more than one year after being let go from that big corporate job, the place that taught me to be specific, marks the time I noticed that everything happens for a reason. Let's recap the story: In the spring of 2016, I was hired to work for one of the largest manufactures of airplanes, a company that when I found out I was going to work for them, I was super happy and super excited to be more financially stable. Turns out I was fired a couple hours after my first day . . . The reason? Unfortunately, because my school would conflict with the hours of the job, as I explained in the chapter titled "Be specific." At the time that it happened, I was crushed . . . And for anybody that truly knows me, it's hard for something to crush me. I have feelings, yes, but I'm a very positive guy and a true believer that everything can change. I knew I would be okay and I would get back on my feet, but it was hard at first to get back up as I felt horrible about what happened.

Later when I got back up, I applied for whatever I found online, such as marketing, salesman, health insurance, anything. I went on multiple interviews and was even offered a job, but I decided it wasn't what I wanted to do. Later I decided to apply to work for an airline, for a position as a Customer Service Agent, which was something I'd done in the past and I had really liked. I applied, and within about a week I was called for an interview. I got the job. Everything happened so fast. Shortly I was flying out of the country for training.

Working at this airline is when I truly started to see that everything happens for a reason. Not only I was able to grow so much in this company, the job had offered me something I always wanted to do in my life: travel. I got to visit a couple places in the US, some even just for a day or two simply because the tickets were practically free (Yes, I went to New York and Washington DC just for one day). I got to go to Europe and have one of the best trips of my life so far, which was something I always wanted to do but it was never within my reach. In addition to traveling, I was also able to focus on school since the job didn't conflict with my classes. I got to finish my Associate's degree a little faster and got accepted into Florida Atlantic University for my Bachelor's in Psychology. If you consider that I was let go from that corporate job because of having a conflict with my school schedule, being able to get my first diploma was extremely rewarding to me. Even more so when you consider that I actually offered to the employer at the corporate job that I would drop my classes at the time just so I could keep that job. But my destiny didn't want that for me, it wanted me to get out of there. Although that job would have had changed my financial life drastically during that time, I wasn't meant to stay there. When I took into consideration that I was meant to stay in school and finish my Associate degree at the time in order to get transferred to a University and started on my Bachelors and travel while doing that, that's when I noticed that everything truly happens for a reason.

Have you ever had a moment like that in your life? Sometimes things happen in our lives that we might not understand it at first. We might think that its cruel and we become upset about it. But if we take a step back and try to understand it, we can actually start to see that it might have happened for a reason, and sometimes a good reason.

14: Problems

"Under this pressure, under this weight, we are diamonds taking shape" – Chris Martin

We all have problems. Even the most peaceful, or successful people in the world have problems. What most people don't realize is that problems are only as bad as you make them out to be.

Sometimes you might feel like everything is going wrong, and you don't know how to make it better. One thing that many of us don't realize is that problems are only as bad as we make them out to be. If you put it in your head that this certain thing that is going on in your life can actually be solved, your problems won't seem as big anymore.

I read an article somewhere about this psychologist that was giving a speech, and he asked everybody how heavy they thought the water cup that he was holding was. The audience started to shout out different weights. However, the psychologist said that the cup was only as heavy as the amount of time he actually holds it up for. So, if he holds it up for a few hours, his arm would start to get tired. Hold it for a day, and he might even feel pain. And so on. Problems work the same way. The longer you keep holding them, the heavier they will be!

So always remember, that nothing is impossible, a problem you have can be solved. Sometimes they might take a little longer to do so, but that's just because life has its speed. Problems are only as bad as you make them, and the longer you hold onto them, the heavier they become! Therefore, we should learn to let go of our problems. I'm not saying that you should find a way to forget them and move on. Doing that will only cause them to get pushed away, making them larger when we have to deal with them again. I mean let go of the weight of that problem. Even if the situation is huge, we can always find a way to overcome it. Sometimes, the results are not exactly what we want, but if it means we can learn something from it, then it is better to have a problem in the first place.

So, let go of the mentality that you "don't understand why this is happening to you" or that "you don't know how you will overcome it." Once you stop thinking that way and start developing a sense of letting go of the weight of the problems, you will have a clearer mind and will be more capable of finding a resolution for it. Under all your problems, there's your normal life. . . never lose sight of it.

15: Can you see past the moment?

"Life is like riding a bicycle. To keep your balance, you must keep moving"
– Albert Einstein

We go through millions of things in our daily lives. Our minds are constantly thinking about how to adapt or react to certain situations. Either an accident on your way to work that might make you late, or a fight between you and a loved one. All these things and more affect our days, and most of them happen out of nowhere, and we might not know what to do. But can you see past the moment?

I've been with my girlfriend for seven years now. We are high school sweethearts that are learning to be adults together. We have our fights like all couples have, some worse than others. Throughout the ups and downs, one day I realized that she is the one I want to be with. I realized that it doesn't matter how bad a fight is, she's the one I want to spend my life with. That's how I came up with this chapter. One day, we had a horrible fight, and I thought that maybe we wouldn't recover from it. But then I took a step back and looked at the situation differently. I realized that no matter how bad it was, I still loved her. Therefore, I started to see past the moment. I started to see life past that fight. If you can do that, then that tells you that a fight is okay to happen, and whatever it is you guys were fighting over can be fixed. Eventually, you will work on whatever you have to work on to fix it and she will as well. That's only if both of you guys can see past the moment.

Now, take this example and use it with everything else that life throws you. Maybe you crashed your car, and you are pissed about it. Or you're having financial issues. Anything. If you take the problem you are having and see life past the moment, you start to feel optimistic about the situation, making you want to work harder to fix it. Many things will knock us down. However, it is the choice to keep moving forward and the choice of seeing the light at the end of the tunnel that gets us through.

Most things in life can be fixed. Some take longer to do so, and others we have little control over such as a sickness, but it's very important to see past the bad moments to help us stay optimistic for the things we care about. So, can you see past the moment?

16: Water your lawn

Many of us go through our lives complaining about things we have, wishing maybe they were different, or maybe wishing we could change them. Things such as our jobs or our relationships. Sometimes we are in a good job or with an amazing partner, but we still find things to complain about. We wish our partners were more loving, respectful, etc. Or sometimes we have a job that we take for granted. We put our emotions into believing that maybe it would be better to move on and look for somebody else, or something else. However, we should consider that the grass isn't always greener on the other side.

Richard & Kristine Carlson, authors of the book *Don't Sweat the Small stuff - in Love*, explain how people are always looking at the negative things that their partners have, and thinking that maybe somebody else would be different. What people are forgetting is that we are all humans, and none of us are perfect. Meaning, you might find somebody else that may be more loving, but maybe that other person won't care as much about your goals as the other partner did. Or vice versa. We all have looked at our relationships like that at least once, maybe during a bad time of it, totally forgetting that nobody is perfect.

The same goes for many other things in our lives. Many people have amazing jobs, at amazing companies, and they still find things to complain about. They wish their superiors gave them more opportunity to grow, or they wish the pay were better. If you consider that maybe you can get a better opportunity for growth if you seek it out, or consider taking advantage of speaking to your manager about growing within the company, maybe your superiors will see that you're worth that raise.

Don't get me wrong, we don't always have a dream job, but that doesn't mean that you can't do your best while you're there to leave your best image behind. We can at least be grateful we have a job in the first place. Also, not all companies will have an opportunity for growth, but it doesn't mean that you should try any less as you never know what can happen the next day! Furthermore, this doesn't apply to relationships where there might be any kind violence or any other kind of deal breakers. However, I do believe that there are many things we can grow past if our partner shows that he or she still cares about making it work.

One of my favorite YouTubers, Richard Williams, more known for his stage name Prince EA, summarized this idea the best way in one of his videos titled "Why You Shouldn't End Your Relationship." Instead of always wondering if there might be somebody or something out there better for you, consider working with what you have, consider all the great things it has brought you, and water your own lawn!

17: What's your mission?

"It's our own ability to have an idea, go after
the idea, and make it happen. That's what at
the end of the day defines us."
– Satya Nadella

What if we can all find our missions here on
earth? What if we can find what we are destined to do?
We should.

Most companies in the world have a mission
statement. That statement doesn't consist of selling as
many units as they can, that statement consists of what
they truly want to accomplish with their services and
products. For example, Microsoft's mission statement as
of 2017 is "empower every person and every organization
on the planet to achieve more." Their statement consists
of more than simply how much they wanted to make, it
consists of what they want to pass on to their customers
through their computers and software. Obviously they

want to be profitable along the way, but their mission consists of what they want to achieve while being profitable.

How many of us have our own mission in life? Our own statement that we want to pass on to other people? To some of us, that mission will one day click, and to others, we might live our lives day by day looking for it. The importance of a mission in our lives is to be aware of the things we care about, the things we are doing, and what motivate us to keep on pursuing them. Microsoft wants their products and services to empower everyone to achieve more. When they see their customers using the computers and programs to achieve more, that's when as a company, they are proud of what they have done, and they are motivated to keep doing more.

So, how do we find our mission? That will come within you! What kinds of things do you like? Are you an outgoing person? Do you like spreading some sort of energy through products or through a simple conversation? What's your talent? Like I said, one day, that mission will come to you. You will wake up and realize what you are intended to do, or maybe an opportunity will present itself, and you might have to react a certain way, and that might determine what you are truly destined to do. The important thing is for us to seek out what our hearts are telling us to do, and go after it.

Your mission should be something your passionate about. To some of you, it will be a career, and that can be anything from being an architect to a gardener. If it makes you happy, you should pursue it. To others, it might be accomplishments such as traveling the world, so that you can learn about cultures and pass that along to others. After all, it's your mission, so it should be what matters to you.

I have truly found my mission statement. I want to spread positivity and empower people to be happier. Yeah yeah, it might sound cliché, right? The thing is, I have realized that choosing to pursue psychology came to me because of my personality. I truly wanted to help people better themselves while at the same time help myself be a better person. In the midst of pursuing this mission of mine, I decided to write this book, which is one step towards that goal of helping others better themselves. At the end of my life, what truly will make me happy and accomplished is to have made people happier and more motivated for life, by spreading a good energy.

We all have a mission; even big companies have one to help them improve and reach their goals. Some of us know what that mission is, others don't. Open yourself to find out what your mission is, and once you find it, chase that idea, and make it happen, as it is what will truly make you happy when you look back on your life.

18: Do what you love

"You've got to find what you love... Your work is going to fill a large part of your life, and the only way to be truly satisfied is to do what you believe is great work, and the only way to do great work is to love what you do."
— Steve Jobs

That's it. Do what you love. Don't pursue a career in something just because it might be easier to finish it. Or because you think that what you actually like, might not be worth pursuing. By doing what you love, happiness and success will always be there.

Hopefully by now you have realized how these chapters connect with one another. Although each one provides a different lesson, all of them lean towards the same goal of self-growth and self-development. This chapter is one of the cores for reaching that ultimate goal.

Some people think that what you do doesn't matter, as long as it makes you successful. Others do things they dislike simply because they think their dreams are too hard to follow. People keep jobs that they think are "secure," then later they end up losing them in the middle of their lives. Now they have wasted their time with something that they didn't love when they could have "wasted" their time being in the field that they are passionate about. The comedian Jim Carrey in a speech he gave at the Maharishi University of Management graduation in 2014, explains that his father could have been a great comedian, but instead chose a secure job as an accountant. Later on, his father lost that job and their family had to do whatever they could to survive. Jim says, "you can fail at what you don't want, so you might as well take a chance in doing what you love."

Doing what you love opens the door to many things such as happiness and a much greater success. People think that being successful will make them happy. However, as explained in a later chapter, happiness is not a destination. Choosing success over happiness will only make you less successful and less happy in the end. Do what you love, be happy, and you will more successful at everything you do. Despite what anybody says, and what anybody thinks, we must always do what we love. No matter how hard it could be, chase your passions. Life is fuller when we are pursuing what we love.

19: Break the cycle

Part of proceeding and progressing is learning how not to be an imitation. When we were little, we learned how to do things by imitating others. Although that is a great method of learning when we are younger, there comes a time in our lives where we have to stop being an imitator and strive to break the cycle.

Sometimes to do what we love, we have to avoid the negative comments others have about what we want to do. We have to be fearless and pursue what we are passionate about even if others don't believe we can do so. Also, we have to learn not to follow the steps of those that weren't successful in pursuing the same things we want to accomplish.

One of my first essays in college was about this very topic: breaking the cycle, and not being an imitator. I was struggling to find what to write about, so my professor approached me and said I should write about something that I truly cared about. At the time, I was living away from home, and my parents' divorce was still hard to deal with since I barely saw them. Therefore, I decided to write about divorce. I wrote about how in life we can either be in imitation of those around us, or we can break the cycle. Having a family has always been something I looked forward to. It's not because my parents went through a divorce, that I want that to happen to me. I must learn from their mistakes and do my best to break the cycle.

The moral of this story can be applied to many other things, not only just a divorce. In the example from the chapter before, the comedian Jim Carrey, explained that his father could have been a comedian, but chose a more secure route at the time. It is not because Jim's father wasn't a comedian that he couldn't be one himself. Another situation can be how sometimes we might grow up in a lower-class family, but that doesn't necessarily mean you have to be poor the rest of your life. I know many artists, musicians, and business people that grow up in a lower-class family and were still able to break the cycle for themselves as they grew other.

So, I believe we can all break the cycle from any situation we are put in. Sometimes it might be harder to do so, or we might make mistakes along the way, trust me, I've made plenty myself. However, when we choose to break the cycle and not be an imitation of those around us, mistakes are only reminders of what truly matters to us, providing us a lesson to move forward. Choose to break the cycle. Similar to the chapter of not being afraid, don't let others tell you that you can't do something. In addition, don't let an environment or a situation you are in discourage you from what you want. Don't be an imitation.

20: Vibration

It's crazy how everything in our lives really does happen for a reason. You can lose a job to follow a better opportunity for you, or how we can be in the right place at the right time.

At the beginning of 2016, I was taking a Biology course that was a requirement for my Associates Degree. The class was challenging because the topic was a bit tough for me. However, the teacher made it possible for everybody to pass the class by providing extra credit and three presentations. Although the topics of the presentations could be literally about anything, most people chose to talk about something related to Biology. On the last week of school, while we were still doing presentations, this guy walked up and decided to talk about the law of vibration. He played a YouTube video by Bob Proctor, which explained the law of vibration. The student later explained that he wanted his presentation to be meaningful, as he wanted to tell us the importance of spreading our good vibrations to others. I was fortunate to be in the right place, at the right time, to be presented to this content.

I was so fascinated by the video that I went home and searched it on YouTube to watch it again. Bob Proctor explained how everything has a vibration, including trees, cement, light, nature, and ourselves. He explained how the vibration we are in is going to determine the things we attract into our lives.

Later, I started to notice the vibration of things. I noticed that when I worry about things too much that it makes me negative, this negativity can bring negative things into my life. I also I started to notice that when I'm in a good mood, and I transfer that mood to others, I can bring more positive things into my life. This law is similar to the law of attraction, as we depend on good vibrations to attract good things in our lives. In a previous chapter, we spoke about how wishing for things, like Aladdin, helps us attract these things. Along with wishing for these things and believing they can happen, we have to be in good vibrations to attract more and more good vibrations into our lives. Understanding the importance of being in a good vibration can help you stay positive during bad moments, and therefore, it allows good things to happen to you.

The same way that everyone and everything has a meaning in this world, as discussed in a previous chapter, there are vibrations for everyone and everything in this world. Therefore, we should seek to be in environments where we can feel good about ourselves. Don't go to places where you don't feel good in it, just because you want to fit in. Don't hang out with people that bring you down, just because you "know" them, and you feel like it's your job to hang out with everybody. These things and more are what bring our vibrations to a negative level, making us mentally exhausted to pursue the things we want in our lives. I'm not saying you shouldn't try to go to unfamiliar places or meet new people. What I'm saying is that if you know you're not a party person, you shouldn't try to go out every weekend just to fit in, and you shouldn't make the effort to hang out with all your friends or people you know if you guys don't necessarily do the same things, but you can still respect them when you see them as you would with any other person.

We all have bad moments, and bad situations, but if we try keeping our minds free and full of good energy by being in a good vibration, that's what we shall receive back.

21: Rollercoaster

Life is made of moments that come and go, moods that can change in seconds, and plans that can suddenly be altered based on things that happen to us. It is one big rollercoaster that goes up and down, so we must buckle up and enjoy the ride.

As I explained in the introduction of this book, much of my inspiration to study psychology and to write about self-development happened when I read the book by Richard Carlson – *Don't Sweat the Small Stuff.* However, there was something else in my life that gave me this passion for writing. In my senior year of high school, my English teacher gave us an assignment that would last all year long. We had to write journals every day during the first 10 minutes of class. The journals could be about anything. You could write about your life, you could write poems, or you could even rap songs. Whatever you wanted to write, you could. What made me comfortable was that he said he would never read your journals, he said he would just skip through the dates and make sure you did it, and that way you would get credit for it. At first, I didn't know what to write, and I thought it was a silly assignment. But as we progressed through the year, I enjoyed more and more the first 10 minutes of that class. I wrote a lot about my senior year experience, but from time to time I wrote about the world as I saw it. The good and bad. The improvements I thought it could have. I was no expert. I was just a high school senior that was doing what most seniors were doing. However, that experience developed in me a passion for writing.

By now, you are probably wondering what this story has to do with life being a rollercoaster. Well, everything. Life can be altered based on situations we are put in. Maybe I wouldn't have developed a passion for writing if I hadn't had that teacher. Maybe I wouldn't even be writing this book. That good moment in my life took me here where I am today. Yes, it surely did. I guess I should thank my English teacher from my senior year in high school, for inspiring me to write freely.

Alternatively, bad moments can also alter our lives. We can become sick, or suffer an accident, and then we have to deal with the consequences. Although we all have different issues and we all go through them differently, we all have to go through them, ultimately, changing the course of our lives.

Along with things that can alter our lives, it's important to know that the same way plans can change, moments and moods also come and go. Many people feel that when they are sad, it's going to be everlasting. Or when their happiness goes away too quickly, they don't understand why. It is important to know that moods can also be altered in a matter of seconds. Sometimes things come up and we can go from happy to sad, in a snap of a finger. I mention this because I know so many people, even close friends and family, that are so upset with life, and how unfair it is sometimes. But, when we discover and understand that life has its ups and downs, we become ready to face the challenges, like a rollercoaster. When we are high, we brace ourselves for the downfall, and when we are down, we can't wait to go upwards, as it usually does. The way we deal with these moods shapes our lives, as a specific feeling can alter the way we feel towards a situation or how we feel towards somebody.

Embrace life. Understand that the page can be flipped, be aware that moments and moods can change, and know that everything can be altered by something happening right now. So, buckle up and enjoy the ride of life.

22: Plan. Change. Plan.

"Intelligence is the ability to adapt to change."
– Stephen Hawking

Imagine if you could tell what tomorrow was going to bring you? Would you do something different today? I'm sure most of us probably would.

The thing is we don't know what tomorrow brings us. As much as we plan our future, it can always change, and all the things that do change can shape our future. As explained in the previous chapter, we are put in situations that can alter our future. Isn't that funny? We can plan, plan, and plan, but we might wake up tomorrow with a situation that is presented to us, that makes us take a different route in our future. The situation could be a sickness, an accident, or just having to move somewhere else, like when I moved to the United States at the age of 12 from a small town in Brazil.

Everything can change, for the good or bad. When I was 17 years old, I bought my first car. I also crashed it within that first year. I thought that car would be in my life for a little bit longer than that, even though it wasn't the car of my dreams. But no. One day I was driving it, and unfortunately, I crashed it. I'm sure something changed in my life somehow because of it. Although it might sound silly, it's true. Maybe the experience I had of crashing my car prevented me from having something worse happen in the future. Or maybe changing my car was what I needed to go through at that moment to learn about how to save money. Sometimes we don't know why something happens, but it does alter something in our lives. Although it wasn't in my plans to change cars within that same year, my plans changed.

This isn't another chapter about how life has its ups and downs, and that we should be able to deal with them. This chapter is to acknowledge that although life can be altered, it doesn't mean it shouldn't be planned. We have to plan our lives, but when alterations happen, such as a car crash, a loss of a job, or a sickness, we have to move forward. We come up with a new plan. Until it changes again, and we come up with a new one again.

Even though we don't know what tomorrow brings us, we must still make our plans, being aware that delays and alterations are always ahead. These changes can sometimes bring valuable lessons. Be prepared for the changes in your life and deal with what they can bring. It is not because things can change that we shouldn't think about our future. The way we deal with changes is what defines us. Be ready to make plans, after plans, after plans, as life is always changing. Deal with it.

23: Happiness

Happiness. What is so hard to understand about happiness? What most people fail to understand is that happiness is not a destination, it's a mood. As you learned from the last few chapters, things can change, including our moods. So why can't we appreciate being happy?

The reason why we are never fully happy is that we look at happiness as a destination, and not a mood. We believe that we will be happy when we land that promotion, buy that new car, renovate our home, or go on a vacation. We are always looking forward to being happy after we get to a certain place in our lives. We count the days for a vacation, so we can be happy. We look forward to getting more money in our jobs to buy new things. We are always looking at happiness as a destination, and that's the problem.

In the book, *The Happiness Advantage*, the author Shawn Achor, explains that happiness actually fuels success. If we are happy first, we become more focused on our goals, making them easier to reach, simply because we are happy. If we look at happiness as a destination, the process to get to it becomes exhausting and everlasting. One example that Shawn Achor gives relating this phenomenon is the following: "If we believe we will be happy if we reach a certain sales target at our job, the moment we reach that target, we will create new ones shortly after, and since happiness was on the opposite side of that success, we push it away even further. If we choose to be happy first and understand that happiness is just a mood that comes and goes and not a destination, we learn to appreciate the times we are happy. Making the weight of our problems a little lighter."

We are all humans. We all have bad moments and bad things that happen to us. I'm sure that even Shawn Achor, who spent years studying positive psychology can agree that sometimes we wake up on the wrong side of the bed and that there are some things that can't be controlled. However, we have the choice to be happy and appreciate the happy moments. We must understand that happiness is not always here. We will encounter moments where we will question why this certain thing is happening to us. We must never forget that moods can change, and whatever we are going through can change as well. In addition, we can choose to be happy first. We can choose to be happy before getting that job or buying that new car. We don't need to let happiness be something that we will only get once we reach a specific destination. Happiness is a mood, such as being miserable, angry, or tired. It will come, and it will go. But we can choose to appreciate it when it's here and not always look forward to it.

24: You can do anything

I told you that I find meaning in most things in my life, right? Have you heard the song by Eminem called "Lose Yourself"? The rapper said a simple sentence in that song that forever changed my life. The sentence is, "You can do anything you set your mind to, man." He wasn't even rapping when he said that, he just said it right at the end, before the song finished. But it forever changed my perspective on success.

After Eminem rapped about his life story, of choking at a rap battle with vomit on his sweater from his mom's spaghetti, the song comes to a conclusion with the rapper saying that you can do anything you set your mind to. While for many, it could be a simple sentence, for me, it gave me a sense of power, and from that moment on, I became more optimistic every time I thought of the sentence. Eminem basically explains that throughout all his struggles, he eventually found a way through by being persistent, and if you set your mind to something, you can find a way to achieve anything you desire.

I spoke about not being afraid; how sometimes even our loved ones can discourage us from the things we want. I spoke about breaking the cycle; how we can't let an environment or the people we surround ourselves with discourage us from what we want. Now, aside from fear and following other footsteps, another reason we often don't pursue things is simply that we think they are too hard.

This is not our parents and friends saying it's too hard, this is our mind saying it's too hard. That's right. How many times have you chosen not to try things simply because you believe it's not worth it or that it's too hard? I could sit here and write a book just about the things I sit around and complain about in my mind every day. We often blame others for not being able to do something ourselves such as how I sometimes blame my girlfriend that I slept too long when I wanted to wake up earlier and be productive. When the truth is, I didn't wake up because I was lazy and I wanted to sleep in a little more. We blame others for not being able to learn a certain task or skill. We complain we don't have enough time. The list goes on. The truth is, we are capable of so much, and yet we choose to do the minimum. We must learn to analyze the things we really want and go after them. Don't just wish for them, go after them.

For many years, I've been telling myself that I would write a book one day. The thought of putting it together and finishing already would be an accomplishment for me. It's been almost five years since I started writing down my thoughts. When I turned 24, I realized that I had enough content and that I should start putting the book together. I always thought I would go a get a Ph.D. and then publish my first book. However, I noticed that the things I was writing about were about my mentality as of now; therefore, I decided it should be published now. I decided that I would publish it by the time I turned 25, as it would mark the first quarter of my life. Maybe it is not the only book I will ever publish. However, these ideas were of my mentality as a young adult, so I knew it was only right to publish it now, and not when I had a Ph.D. Although I still plan to pursue a higher education, I knew that this book couldn't wait until then.

The point is, my story proves that you can do anything you set your mind to. Nobody told me to write a book. I just set my mind that I wanted to do that, and I did. What is it that you want to do? Don't just wish for it, go after it. Sometimes we don't do things because of the fear that others put on us, but other times, we don't do it simply because we don't put our minds into it. So, put your mind to something, and chase it. You will be happy that you did so.

25: Be positive

Why are people so negative? Life is so beautiful, yet we find ways to be negative. We are always creating barriers in our lives based on the adversity that we face, causing us to be negative. We must learn to be positive through the ups and downs and face our adversities.

One of the most important things we need to do in life to be happy is to be positive. Be positive with yourself, for yourself. As long as we are positive today and positive for tomorrow, we can always achieve what we want. Don't forget that the law of vibration and law of attractions exists for a reason. Just as long as you believe that it can always get better, it will. I learned with Richard Carlson that things that happened to us now might be totally forgotten in a couple of years. Concerns we have now, might not be as important later. So why must we stress over all of them? After all, things change, but as long as we are positive, we can always change them for the better.

The following two chapters will talk about positivity. You will learn that you can't just be positive and that you have to feel positive! However, the ultimate goal is to BE POSITIVE. Learn from challenges and changes. Enjoy life being positive, and positive things will come to you.

26: Don't just be positive

"You cannot just exist in this life. You have
got to try to live. . . but to get to that life,
you're going to have to jump." – Steve Harvey

Being positive is very important for us to be able
to proceed and progress into a better life. However, we
can't just be positive, we must act on it.

This chapter is very important to this book. By
now, I hope you have gained some of the positive energy
I'm trying to spread with my thoughts. I mentioned how
things change on the rollercoaster of life, how everything
happens for a reason, and how we must wish for the
things we want. However, many people rely only on faith
and positivity to get to where they want in life.

Many people I know suffer from this issue.
Something happens in their lives, and they choose to just
maintain positive in order to move on. Or they wish to do
something, but they believe that just by being positive, it

will happen to them. While being positive is hugely important, we must learn to act on it.

Acting on it is a simple as picking up your computer and starting to write the book you said you wanted to write. If you want to do something, you have to start doing it. Bob Proctor in his book *The ABC's of Success* said, "Change your life today. Don't gamble on the future, act now, without delay." Being in a good vibration, along with wishing for your dreams to come true, has an enormous impact on actually making them come true. But, if you don't act on it, nobody will do it for you. The process is done step by step. Even the smallest steps move you that much closer to making your dreams and goals come true. It's not just about wishing and hoping one day you can get to where you want. It's about putting the work in. It's about putting effort into something you care about even after long hours at work. It's about finding ways to get it done. It's about doing it.

Start now. Chase your dreams and your passions, and while doing so, be positive that you can get to where you want, and you will.

27: Feel positive

"You can't live a positive life with a negative mind." ~ Prince EA

Similar to being positive, it is important to feel positive. People show that they are positive about many things in life. Especially now with the internet and social media, people portray that everything is good in their life. They want to show that they are positive and that great things are happening. But do they actually feel positive?

To feel positive is to understand that bad things happen and to know that you can overcome them. It's not about what you show, it's about what's truly inside of you. What do you really feel? Can you overcome an obstacle that comes your way? Can you overcome a barrier that stops you from reaching your goals? Feeling positive is about knowing that you can get where you want in life no matter how hard it gets.

Similar to seeing past the moment, feeling positive is imagining yourself achieving that goal even if it's hard to do so. Sometimes you want to make more money, but you feel stuck in a company that you might not see yourself growing in. Or you want to do something in your life, but there are barriers that stop you from doing so. Feeling positive is about seeing past the moment and truly feeling positive. It's not about what you portray to others, it's about having a true sense of positivity within you. Life will bring many alterations, and some of these alterations won't be what we desire, but we must have a sense of positivity within us to find the strength to keep going.

When we learn how to feel positive, we become more positive people. We end up portraying positivity to others without trying so hard to do so. Simply because we feel positive. When we engage in positive feelings, we receive positive things in our lives. So, don't just act positive or portray positive things to others, you must feel a positive energy within yourself in other to attract more great things in your life.

28: 10 years

Ever stopped to think where your life will be in 10 years? Have you accomplished the goals you set? Did you become the person you wanted to become?

Not everybody has goals for 10 years. But if we stop to think about it, it's very important to do so. If you can't imagine for things you want to accomplish 10 years from now, at least stop to think if the you from 10 years from now would be proud of you today. Or do you think the you from 10 years from now would see today differently? Would you change some of your habits to get where you want to be? Would the you from 10 years from now be proud of you, or disappointed with the decisions you took?

Take a moment to think about this. Take a deep breath and think about these questions. Are you happy? What would you change? Looking ahead helps us focus not only on what we want to achieve, but it also helps focus on what we are doing right now.

Do this often. As you proceed with your life, your goals might change, your circumstances might be different. Therefore, it is important to always go back and practice this exercise again and again. Do it right now

. . .

What do you see?

29: What do you look forward to?

We all need something to look forward to. Whatever is in the back of your mind is truly what defines who you are. Do you look forward to what you will do over the weekend? Or do you think more deeply about bigger things, such as having your own house or graduating?

Don't get it twisted. We all have small things we look forward to. We all look forward to a party we might attend or a vacation. But what is it that you truly look forward to? What is that thing that is out of reach right now that you can't wait to go through? It's important to have those big things to look forward to. While for some that might be buying the car of their dreams or their first home. To others, it might be that they look forward to graduating, or opening their own business. When I take a moment to look where my life is going to be in 10 years and the things I look forward to, I look forward to being a great father and an amazing husband. Being a supportive husband to my beautiful wife, by being there and supporting her with her dreams. Helping her accomplish what she wants will make me happy. Seeing my children grow, helping them through all their hard moments, teaching them about life in general. That's what I look forward to. That's truly what I want. I also look forward to being successful in my career. I want to be able to be proud of the things I have done in my field and help as many people better themselves. I also looked forward to publishing this book. I spent countless hours making this dream come true, and now that it is here, I still can't believe I pulled it off. So, I guess that's one thing off my bucket list.

Never stop looking forward to things. Always make goals. As mentioned earlier, our plans and our circumstances may change, that is why it is important to add new things to look forward to. However, never let go of those things that truly matter to you. The things that you think about the most are the things that will make you stronger to keep pushing forward through the hard times. So, once you figure out the big things you look forward to, don't let go of them. The journey to a happier life will be more attainable once you start making those big things a reality.

So, what do you look forward to?

30: Success

I mentioned many things in this book regarding success. I mentioned you should follow your dreams regardless of what others say, and that you should visualize success to keep the focus on what you want. However, what does success mean to you?

In my opinion, success means being happy with fewer worries. It means waking up in the morning to do what you love. It means sharing a life with somebody you love. Many people look at success based on the amount of money they make, the job they have, the car they drive, or the house they live in. However, success shouldn't be measured by the amount of money you have, but by the experiences you collect. Meaning, the more experiences you have in your life, the more successful you shall be. You should be able to share a life of love, with somebody that you feel that is worth going through all the struggles with. You should wake up eventually with fewer worries. And most importantly, you should be able to do what you love, so work doesn't become such a drag. I know we will have jobs along the way that we dislike, we all have to go through that, especially the young adults, whose first job are never usually the one that they choose to do the rest of their lives. But we can still seek to work towards finding what we love. When we start doing what we love, our work becomes an experience that we adore doing.

Choose to do something in your life that is going to make you happy, not something that is going to bring you the most money. If you work for it, money will come eventually. There's nothing more rewarding in life than the experiences you go through, and the best experiences will come when you are doing something that makes you happy.

Not sure what you want to do? No worries, that also comes with time. It will click in your head, and you will notice that you are meant to do that all along! For me, it has been psychology. Sometimes while learning about psychology or reading a book about self-development, I become mesmerized by the content and how it can be applied to my life or the lives of others. I love the topic, and learning about it has become an experience to me.

Find your own meaning of success. Don't let others define it for you. We live our lives worrying about our status—we feel that success is about the car we drive, the house we own, and the money we make. Although those things are important, they shouldn't be what drives you. Find your meaning of success and let that be in the driver seat. Remember, at the end of your life, your money won't matter much, but the experiences you collected will.

31 : M & M

Do you know about the M & M's of life? No, it's not the chocolate, but what better way to make you remember this chapter than to naming it M & M, like the chocolate? The M & M of life are: Miserable and Motivated. I learned that in life, we can be one or the other.

One day, in a work meeting, my manager said that we are either miserable or motivated. We are either miserable or motivated at any place we work. If we are miserable working there, it doesn't necessarily mean we are only miserable there because of the complaints we have about the job. A miserable person will always be miserable in any place they work in. They might find a job that pays more, but they will find other things in that new job to complain about because they are a miserable person. The motivated person, on the other hand, will be motivated at any place he or she works at. They might not like the pay or the role they are in, but the motivated person still does the best that they can, even at the worst job.

I left work that day, and I was fascinated by what I had just heard. I realized that this applies to everything in life, and not just at work. When a miserable person is in a position that they are unhappy about, they will say that the reason their life is the way it is, it's because of the situation that they are in. But stop and think about it . . . Do you really think that the person will change their way of thinking and stop complaining if such situation changed? Do you really believe that the person will now be happier, and a less stressed person if they get what they want? I came to the conclusion that they won't. When you are miserable, it doesn't matter what changes in your life, you will continue to find things to complain and be miserable about. The motivated person, on the other hand, is the person that will come back from something tragic with a story to tell, ready to face the issues, and continue to go on with their lives. The motivated person works their best on any job they are in, even if they don't like the role or the pay they receive.

We have the choice of being either miserable or motivated. When we are miserable, we will continue to be miserable in any given circumstance of our lives. When we move on from what is miserable now, we eventually find something else to be miserable later. When we are motivated, we live our lives to its best, no matter the circumstances we are in. Stop and think which of the M's are you, and if you are miserable, see if that's just a phase. You can only start enjoying life once you let go of being miserable completely. Stop finding things to stress about, stop sweating the small stuff, and start being motivated.

32: Living and leaving

"When my time comes. . . help me leave behind
some. . . reasons to be missed."
– Chester Bennington

What good is living, if you're not actually leaving something behind? Take a moment to analyze the people in your life. Do you think they are living a life where they will feel proud of it in the end? Are you? We go about our days without considering what we would like to leave behind. Some of us just live each day thinking and doing the usual. Is that enough?

Ever wonder if what you are doing or what you have done will be remembered? I spoke about this in the chapter titled "10 Years." However, this is more than looking at your life 10 years from now and accomplishing your goals. This is about what you truly want to leave behind when you're gone. Most of us live our lives without wondering if one day it will matter to someone else. I'm not talking about just your family and loved ones. I'm talking about leaving something behind period. Did you impact someone's life by helping them in a time of need? Did you open the business of your dreams that made an impact on something or someone? We all have goals, and things we want to do; however, few of us think about a legacy we want to leave behind. Take a moment today to identify what is it that you want to leave behind. Question yourself: what do I want to be remembered as? Or what do you want to be remembered for?

I decided to study psychology because of how my characteristics matched the field, and because I wanted to help people. For me, studying to be a counselor wasn't enough. So, I also decided to write this book. I wanted my thoughts to be written, for me and others to read them, in a time of need or for motivation. I made a commitment to write this book and to leave it behind when I'm gone.

I'm sure most of us want to leave something behind, but I'm also sure very few of are doing anything about it. Don't just live day by day. Seek what you love, think about what you need to get there, do your best to accomplish it even if it takes 10 years, and then leave your mark in the world you are in. The truth is that our actions are important, everything we do makes us who we are, and who we are will impact someone's life, and by impacting a person's life, we can be remembered. So, who do you want to be remembered as? There is no better feeling in living and leaving something behind.

33: Nature vs. Nurture

Yeah yeah, the old psychological debate of what creates an identity. If you have taken any psychology course in your life, you have come across this topic. Lately, I've been trying to understand more and more why people are the way are. People being those very close to me, or just any regular human being that comes into my life.

I judge people I work with and wonder why they don't work as hard as me. I judge those around me and the decision they make about themselves and their future. As mentioned in a previous chapter, I believe that judging people is okay. It makes you realize where you stand on the things that matter to you, makes you realize what you're doing is actually good, and makes you focus on what's important. What is not okay is to judge people to their faces or to others. Another reason why is not okay to judge them that way is because of Nature vs. Nurture. Think about it. These people might be lazy at work or make silly decisions about their lives because of what's in their genes (nature). They had no choice. They were born with these genes. In addition, the way they were nurtured by their parents and the environment didn't contribute to changing those genes. Sometimes the individual might not be born with these genes, but the environment they grow up in shapes their identity into being what they are (nurture). So, whose fault is it? The parents!? Maybe . . . possibly. The parents do play a vital role in shaping their children's identity. How a parent reacts to when a child says they want something or don't want something, can definitely determine if that child will grow up to go after things by themselves or wait until it's given to them. Most of the basic personality traits a human acquires when they are young. Theorist Erik Erickson explained in his *Psychosocial Theory* how when children are between three and five years old, they begin to ask many questions as their thirst for knowledge grows. They begin asking "WHY" to explore the world. Meaning, they are seeking answers to things they don't know and looking to the adults around for answers. When you consider that most children will spend most of their times with their parents, the children will nurture many things from them. When you add up the personality traits the children are born with, you can most definitely agree that the parents can have a big impact on their children's way of thinking, such as being lazy at work or making poor decisions. Anyways, I'm not here to just blame the parents. Although I'm not a parent yet, I can most definitely agree how hard it is to be one. The point I'm trying to make is that the nature and nurture of a child together plays a vital role in shaping one's identity.

Many people grow up lacking extrinsic and intrinsic motivation, which is the desire to engage in activities for external reasons or simply because they enjoy them, causing them to have the personalities we see in them. Can it be an issue caused by nature AND nurture? Like I said, I'm not just blaming the parents, but sometimes a person has no choice for the way they act. Understanding this has allowed me to gain a different perspective of how we form personalities, and it has given me the ability to feel more empathy for people around me. Now, instead of always trying to understand why they are lazy at work, I started to notice that maybe that person was given everything when they were kids; therefore, they were shaped into this personality. Next time you start to judge somebody because of something you don't like about them, consider that maybe that person was exposed to a life that made him or her that way. Maybe when considering that, you might have a little more empathy for them, and it will allow you to not fight their ways of being and give you an opportunity to learn to deal with it.

PS: One thing to keep in mind is that how you were raised and by whom you were raised clearly does affect you, but it shouldn't define who you are. You can break out of that, as spoken in the chapter titled "Break the cycle." However, your nature and nurture will still be with you, but it can be less noticeable if you realize that it does affect you and you make the decision to change.

34: Oversharing

It's 2018, where we have smartphones, tablets, smartwatches, and more. We use technology for everything. Are we using it too much to share our lives?

The more ways we have to interact with technology, the more ways we have to share our lives online. Social media is a big trend. People are always sharing what they are doing around the world by posting pictures and hoping to get as many "likes" as possible. Although social media has been an excellent tool that allows us to connect with our friends and family across the globe, it is important to know how to control it.

I think many of us suffer from one simple disorder, the oversharing disorder. It means exactly that; we share too much. We have to control what is necessary to share and the amount we share. I read an interesting article one day from an author I cannot recall, talking about how couples that share less online are happier. And it's true. The couples that crave less attention from others have a much healthier relationship. With fewer people wondering about how good they are, they are able to focus on making themselves happier. When I started going out with my girlfriend, I always wondered why she wouldn't post anything about us like most girls our age. I even wondered if she was ashamed of me or something.

(I was 18 years old at the time, so don't judge my insecurity). I questioned her about it, and she told me the relationship is ours, are we are the ones that need to know about it. Now I know that by not oversharing our lives we are only strengthening our relationship.

I'm not going to lie. I still love to share pictures of something cool I'm doing such as a vacation, or a message that I think it's important. However, I learned that it doesn't need to be everything, and especially every day. You have something to say, then say it, but make sure it is necessary. Take a moment before posting something and see if you really need to share that picture or that status.

Here are three things to consider why it is important not to overshare. First, not everybody cares. You might think they do, but they don't. They might just scroll through your post, or simply read something you thought was important and completely forget about it later. Second, there are people out there who might be jealous of you and capable of doing things to hurt you. Finally, once you start oversharing, it can be hard to go back on it. Meaning, you might end up having to explain why something didn't work out later.

Given these points, it is fair to say, don't overshare! The world doesn't need to know about you and the silly things you do every day. The people that matter the most to you can be contacted in other ways. You can still post stuff but make sure that your post is necessary, as there is a big difference in sharing and oversharing.

35: Choices

We have a choice for everything that happens in our lives. This might sound crazy, but it's true. Every opportunity that arises is based on a choice we had to make. The mood we are in is based on a choice we made to be in that mood. The things that happen to us are based on a choice we made leading to that.

Crazy right? Tal Ben-Shahar, author of the book *Choose the Life You Want,* explains that everything is based on a choice. If we are given a job opportunity or a promotion, we have to make a choice to go for it or not. If we are in a bad mood, we can choose to either stay in that mood or let go of it. If something bad happens to us, such as a divorce, we probably were given choices leading up to it such as to be better. It's understandable that some things in our lives we have no control of it such as the death of a loved one or an injury, but even those situations, we have the choice of how long we will grieve for, or how long we will let our injury hold us back.

When we choose to move on from being upset, we choose to accept opportunities, and much more. When I was let go from that big corporate job after my six-hour shift, I was crushed. For some time, I had no idea what to do. I had no job and had my bills to pay. Fortunately, with time I began understanding that I had to move on. So, I made a choice to move on. I started doing Uber until I found another job. Eventually, I changed my mood from being upset and started being me again, and things started falling back into its place. The reason I bring up the moment I was fired from that job again it's because it was a bad moment of my life. However, I made the choice to move past it, and pick up the pieces.

There's always a choice to be made: the choice of being a good employee; the choice of committing to a task; the choice of being a good husband or wife; the choice of being a good student; and the choice of moving on after a loss of a job or a loved one. However, we don't always make the right choices, and that's okay. We are only human, and we make mistakes. But after the mistake has happened, don't forget that you have the choice of moving on, and the choice of learning from what happened.

We are in control of our lives. If something is holding you back, make the choice of finding an alternative solution. Always make the choice that will lead to a better you, even if sometimes there are misleading paths along the way. Choose to proceed and progress with your life. Choose to be happy.

36: Plan A

This book was always intended to share a positive energy with others and to show others how to better people through my perspective. Most of my topics share a similar idea, and although I don't want to sound too repetitive, I have yet another reason why we should always be positive. How many times were you in a situation that you decided to make a *Plan B* in case *Plan A* didn't work out? We all want to avoid stress and downfalls, so much so that we plan an escape route in case something happens to *Plan A*. But what if I told you sometimes it's bad to have a *Plan B?*

In the book *Before Happiness* by Shawn Achor, he talks about how people are always looking for escape routes. We find ourselves spending time planning an alternative in case something goes wrong. What we really should do is spend time being positive about what we truly want. For example, instead of wondering what you will do if you do bad on an interview for a job, focus more on how you can do great on it, or how you can improve your impression on the employer. So many people do this, I mean, so many! We probably all have done it. It's hard not to. We want everything to be good, so we look ahead to prevent things from going bad. Shawn Achor explains that spending time finding escape routes might actually turn them into reality. That's right, now those escape routes are real! Remember the law of attraction? Well, concentrating your mind on finding an alternative will only make you attract that alternative route, which can make you less focused on *Plan A*, making it less attainable for you.

Some of you might be thinking, "at least I was prepared for it." Truthfully, those routes can always be there. You don't know what tomorrow will bring you. You might have an alternative option for a job in case you don't get the job you're applying for today; however, tomorrow your alternative job might close down . . . After all, life is full of surprises, and things can change. So why focus on what we should do in case something goes wrong when we actually don't know what tomorrow will bring? What we should do is focus on being positive at all times with the things that we actually want. Instead of worrying about not getting that job, focus on how you can nail that interview! Instead of worrying about what you will do if you fail your test, concentrate on finding more time to study for it. It might seem hard to do it at first, but when you can start focusing on what you actually want to accomplish it, you won't need your *Plan B* anymore.

Go with *Plan A*, that's always the best route. Focus on achieving it. If it doesn't work, see if there any way to try it again. Be persistent. Don't give up easily on the things you truly want. *Plan B* can always be arranged later if you actually need it. *Plan A* is what truly matters.

37: Face your fears

As mentioned in a previous chapter, we all have fears. We fear not fitting in, fear of doing things we have never done before, or fear of spiders. Facing our fears might be hard, but it can turn out to be very rewarding.

When I moved to the United States, I had a major problem in school. Since English wasn't my first language, I wasn't comfortable speaking it out loud. I hated every time I had to read for the entire class, or when I had to do a presentation. I would panic when a teacher would say we would "play" popcorn. Popcorn is when we start reading something such as a novel or a short story and the student reading it must pick the student that will read afterward. My anxiety would kick at the moment we would start. I would start sweating in anticipation of my turn. That was probably the worst thing ever! I never knew when I was going to be picked to read! Aside from the fact that I already didn't enjoy reading it out loud, I hated not knowing when my turn would be. It's not like you can avoid being picked, especially when I had classes with my best friend Rafael, and he would pick me on purpose. Because that's what friends do (laugh out loud). I hated everything about that "game," and for that reason, I thought I hated reading out loud.

Later when my English improved, I would still be nervous during those situations. I didn't know if it was because of the English language itself or if it was just me afraid of public speaking. One day I realized I had to get rid of that fear, so I decided to look at it from another perspective: I decided to always volunteer to read or do my presentation first, that way instead of looking nervous, I looked confident, and that would boost my morale. It helped. I discovered that I like public speaking, and I'm passionate about speaking in front of others and expressing my opinion.

Will Smith gave an excellent example of fear during an interview in 2016. He mentioned how before skydiving, he got scared the night before, until the moment he was on the door of the airplane. But when he jumped out, he discovered the blissful experience that flying was. Will mentions that there is no reason to be afraid before the event and that we should have been afraid only when we are "flying." However, we react the opposite way. We let the fear take over us prior to the specific event even happening. The same way how I would be petrified of reading prior to even starting to. Will said, "God placed some of our most blissful moments on the other side of terror or our maximum fear." An amazing quote from an amazing person.

The point is, life will give you tough situations, and the way you go through it is by looking at it a different way, and analyzing how you can change it. Don't let the fear take over, face it, it might turn out to be something you truly enjoy doing.

38: Everybody is equal

Don't ever feel above anybody . . . even if you are. Having a role that is maybe above somebody in a job, or having more than somebody, doesn't mean you should make them feel as if you're above them. What will make you more successful and happier is always making sure that although you might technically be above somebody in a job or financially, you should always treat everyone as equal.

People that discourage and mistreat others because they feel like they have more power are sad. I mean it. Do you think that the obsessive person that is constantly showing off their things, and by doing so, make others feel like they are nothing, are better than you? They might be better than you financially, but inside, they are just sad people who need attention. Don't seek attention. If you are successful in your career or financially, don't mistreat people that are below you, instead, encourage them to be like you. Help them find ways to lead them to success. If you can't do that, then at least have some integrity, and don't bring them down. Nobody likes a person that makes others feel less of themselves. Nobody likes a boss that overreacts just because he or she has the power to do so. Be a leader. Stay humble even if you are the boss. Make others want to follow you. That's what will differentiate you from a boss to a leader. We all had that one superior that thinks they are better than us simply because they are in a role of power. I can't imagine how many times I knew something that a superior person at my workplace had no clue about it. It does mean I'm better than them neither. This just goes to show to everybody can be equal. This shouldn't apply only to skills, but morals as well. Don't be the superior that shows power just because you can, be the leader others want to follow. Don't be the leader that misuses their power. Don't be somebody that is cocky because you might have something that others don't.

This is so simple yet so complex. Many people get caught up with success, power, and fame, and they portrait themselves above others. That will only make you sad and with time, people will push you away. Be equal. That is what is more important. That is what the world needs.

39: Make the most of your time

This chapter is short and sweet. However, I needed to fit it in here because it is very important for me to always remember this.

We live our lives worrying, complaining, and rambling about how life is unfair. We waste our times on unnecessary things. We spend time with the wrong people. We pursue things we don't love. Some people do these things more than others. But we all have done at least one of these at some point of our lives. This chapter is not only about the silly things we choose to waste time on it. This chapter is about how life is short, and yet we choose to waste time.

I've seen many stories of people that died at such a young age. We take for granted the time we have in here. We fight with people we love. We complain when things don't go our way. We whine about silly things. Instead, we should choose to take advantage of our lives as much as we can. Travel the world. Meet people. Love people. Don't complain about life as much. Don't whine about silly things.

We worry so much about what needs to be done and what wasn't done properly. Worry less. Stress less. Laugh more. Love more. Life is short. Enjoy it while it lasts.

40: Opinions

We live in a world where we all have our own opinions. We argue and argue about what is right or wrong. Respecting the opinion of others is very important, but never forget to have your own.

We discuss our opinions with our friends, family, co-workers, and loved ones. Sometimes while debating different opinions, we forget the importance of respecting what others believe. We also forget to respect the opinions we have ourselves, simply because we might just give in to what others say. I learned that when I'm having an argument with somebody, or just debating what is right or wrong, I eventually respect their opinions without forgetting mine. Sometimes I simply agree with them by saying, "you're right" while in the back of my mind I'm saying, "well actually I still believe I was right but OK." I have learned to drop the argument and move on, prior to making my mind mentally exhausted debating who is right or wrong. I learned to agree and respect the other person's opinion while still having my own. Not every argument needs to be won. Some just need to be understood.

I noticed that a big problem in friendships and relationships is how we get to a point where we just agree with the other person, simply to move on with the topic, but forget to have our own inner opinions. You might not always need to express them like I mentioned, but it's important to follow what you believe. In some situations, it is important to actually say what you want, even if it causes a conflict with the person you are speaking with. If the person wants you to do something or act a certain way, and you think you need to take a different path, your feelings should always be expressed. If you noticed that during the time of conflict the person is not listening, try mentioning to them what you believe later, when things are more settled. We can't allow others to do things they think is best for us, simply because we want to avoid the argument. In a family, relationship, or in a friendship you must always think the best for the others. However, you can't just think something and assume that's the best thing for them. You have to make sure you understand that the other person also has their opinion on what is best. Stand your ground, listen and understand each other's thoughts and respect them. Or else that family, relationship, or friendship isn't a family, relationship, or friendship.

It is important to have opinions. If the situation is important like a matter of what a family should do regarding whether or not they should move to a new home, then make sure your opinion is heard, even if it is afterward. Now, if the debate is simply about something silly, we can learn to agree with a person simply to drop the subject, but make sure we still stay true to what we believe inside. Opinions sometimes need to be expressed, other times they don't, however, make sure to always have one, while still respecting what the other person stands for.

41 : Enjoy being alone

"The truth about who we are lives in our heart."
– Brené Brown

I believe today more than ever, people don't enjoy being alone. With the rise of social media, we are always seeking the attention of others. Besides the internet, people are always dying to hang out with their friends and family at all times. They feel almost if they are missing out if they are not with them. Although spending time with our friends and loved ones is important, nothing helps us grow more than enjoying the times we are alone.

We take for granted the times we are alone. We waste it by complaining why we are not doing something fun, or why we are not able to be at a specific place. I know people that are always wanting to be with others, even if it's to do nothing. They simply prefer doing nothing with their friends. Although having friendships are important and spending time with them gives us a feeling of affection, the times we are alone is when we are truly connected with ourselves. When we are alone, we are connected with our minds and with our hearts, and we are able to concentrate on the things that truly matter to us. When we are alone is when we can truly stop to think what we want and find ways to get there. Being alone is very important in my life. Those are the times when I can reflect on what's going on today or in general, and see what I can do about it. Those are the times I can plan my future, and make sure I'm taking the proper steps to get there. Sometimes being alone is hard. We might live with our families, and when we are out of the house, we are working, leaving us no time for ourselves. We can always find times for ourselves. Most of my alone time is in the car or when I'm showering. When I have the opportunity to be completely alone in my room or in my house, I take advantage of it. I appreciate being alone, as it gives me an opportunity to hear my mind and my heart.

When we are only focused on being around people and we don't appreciate our time alone, we end up not letting our mind and our heart take its course. We lose the opportunity of letting our mind create great ideas and goals for ourselves. Being alone is one of the things that led me to write this book. So maybe if you start appreciating your times alone, you might come up with something great yourself. Enjoy being alone, as there is no better way to connect with what matters to you.

42: Mind of an adult & heart of a kid

"All children are artist. The problem is how to remain an artist once he grows up."
– Pablo Picasso

As we grow older and gain more responsibility, we come to forget the beauty that it is being a kid. I noticed that in order to live a happier life, we have to learn how to have the mind of an adult and the heart of a kid.

How many times have you seen an old adult complaining about something so silly, or something they have no control of it? Since most of my life I've had jobs in the field of customer service, I have seen many things. At the airport, I've seen parents arguing about the size of the line at customs as soon as they land for their vacation. Reminder: they are on "vacation" and they still choose to start it by complaining about such things. I've seen parents tell their kids to stop having fun even at times that the kids weren't doing anything wrong. I'm not a parent yet, but how silly is it to tell a child not to have fun when they are clearly not disturbing anyone? People should really start listening to Richard and Kristine Carlson, and learn how not to sweat the small stuff. There are things we can't control, and other's not worth fighting about, but because we are adults, we lose our train of thought sometimes and act out in such situations. I have done it. You probably have done it too. However, I learned that to live happier, we have to be responsible like adults are supposed to be, but be loving and free like kids are. Kids laugh at silly things, give unconditional love to those who care for them and enjoy the many things that we adults might take for granted. We grow up so focused on our goals and responsibilities that we forget to enjoy our lives. We have to learn that we are not in this world forever; therefore, we should take some things less serious. We can still be responsible adults while maintaining a sense of humor, while giving attention to those we love, and while not stressing about everything so much.

Happiness, as mentioned in a previous chapter, is a mood like every other mood. So, enjoy it when it is around. Don't stress about the things we have no control of. Give love to those you care about. Laugh at the silly things. Enjoy the benefit of living. We can still be responsible adults, but with a heart of a kid.

43: Decisions

"A man's conflicts represent what he really is."
— Erik Erikson

There are so many decisions to make in life. We decide between different job opportunities, we decide whether we should move to a new place, and we even decide if we should go back to school. These and more are the many things people have to decide in their lives. The key to making any decision is to learn that no decision is a bad decision.

It might be hard to see it at first, but when we learn to appreciate that even a bad decision is a good decision, we look at our loss as an opportunity for growth. Nelson Mandela once said, "I never lose. I either win or I learn." The decisions we make with our lives can either lead us to a win or to a loss. However, when we look at our loss as an opportunity for growth, we learn that mistakes are meant to help us win the next time. We might make a poor decision now that leads us to something terrible, but when we learn from it, we learn that the lost only happened for us to succeed in the future. Most of the times we are not going to agree with what is happening to us, we will say things like "why is this happening" because when we make a bad decision and something doesn't go our way, it does that to us. It is hard to prevent ourselves from not feeling upset in these situations. However, learning to eventually accept our decisions, even the bad ones, helps us make a better decision the next time we are in a similar situation.

Don't be afraid to make decisions, there can always be a win-win situation if looked at the right way. We might not always understand the true meaning at first, but when you consider that everything happens for a reason and that every decision can turn out to bring something positive, we learn to take more chances. We are given decisions in order to shape who we really are. It's hard to choose between different options because what we are really doing is deciding upon the best thing for ourselves. We don't always make the right decisions. A big chunk of them we might not succeed at first, but when we learn that the decision can be used as a chance to grow, we are more prepared to make them.

44: Bad days

"One day, in retrospect, the years of struggle
will strike you as the most beautiful."
– Sigmund Freud

It's easy being positive when things are going well. When we have a steady job, all our bills paid, when we are healthy, etc. The challenge is being positive when thing are not going the way we want. Because that's when we need it the most.

When things are bad, we need to be strong, we need to remind ourselves that this is just a phase, and we need to remember that the page can be flipped. Those that can do that are the true optimistic people. Mastering this skill is not easy, because all of us go through bad moments, days, and situations, and sometimes, depending on the situation, it might be hard to see the light at the end of the tunnel. But if you think about it, how many things have you gone through in your life that you thought were incredibly difficult, and you didn't know how you were going to recover from? Most of us can think of many. But most of those moments have passed, and they are now just a memory of a bad day. I read once that it's okay to have a bad day, as they are what makes the good days more exciting. The same way that happiness is just a mood that changes, being angry or upset can also go away. To understand that is okay to have a bad day, and that everybody has them, is when you truly have mastered being optimistic.

So, whenever you're having a bad day just know that something good is around the corner. Life will bring you a series of ups and downs, but that's what makes it great! After all, if it were all just great all the time, it would be boring. Even if you are going through a situation that will never be forgotten as a horrible moment in your life, hang in there, life can have something great around the corner. One of my favorite motivational quotes is, "life is like an arrow, it pulls you down, in order to shoot you back up." So, be positive, but most importantly, be positive through bad days, because that's when you need it the most. Whatever it is that is bothering you, look at it as an opportunity for growth, and know that the page can always be flipped, because it will.

45: Age is not a job title

People look at age differences as a job title. Some people think that just because they are older, they know more than you and they are more "experienced" than you. This is not always true.

How many times when you were trying to talk to somebody older, and they make you feel like you should do as they said simply because they are older than you? I know I have gone through many moments like that, and you probably have too. Sometimes it happens with our parents, or simply somebody you work with. Some people demand that you do as they said simply because they are older. Don't get me wrong, kids should obey their parents when they are told to do so. However, there are other times when you are not a kid anymore, and you are trying to tell your dad or your older brother to do something a certain way and they act out because they are older and they know what they are doing. People fail to realize that there comes a time that we all have something to learn from one another. A 20-year-old adult can most definitely have gone through a situation that a 40-year-old adult can learn from. And vice versa. Unfortunately, many older folks take knowledge for granted. They look at their age as a job title, as if they have a superior title than you in the career of life. We have to learn how to appreciate everybody's point of view and always listen to what they have to say. Age is just a number, not a job title. An older adult might have experienced more things, but it doesn't mean that the young adult doesn't have anything valuable to add up to a situation or a topic.

When I started putting this book together, my biggest fear was if people wanted to learn about what I had to teach them. So, I thought that I would keep writing this book until I was older with a Ph.D. to publish it. It was not only because of the degree that I thought I needed to publish this book, it was also because I thought I had to be much older in order to have valid information that others would want to learn from it. However, I started to notice that the things I was writing about were related to my young adult life. If I waited until I was older and graduated to publish it would mostly have been changed. Therefore, I made it my goal to publish before I turned 25-years-old as this is a young adult's perspective on self-development. I had to let go of the fear that I wasn't "old enough" or needed to "graduate" to write a book about self-development. I noticed that age was just a number, and that I, too, had valuable lessons to pass on to others, regardless of their age. There was a time where I was doubting myself and the idea of publishing this book at only 25-years-old, but my girlfriend said something that forever changed my life. She said, "when a person comes to you for help, they don't ask your age or your job title in order to seek an opinion. Your age or your degree shouldn't stop you from adding something valuable to a topic you care about." Thank you, my dear.

So, don't let others tell you what to do, or how to do it, simply because they are older. On the other hand, if you are the person that believes others should listen to you just because you are older, stop that. Everybody has different things they go through in their own lives, and a younger person can bring valuable information to a topic as well. Age is not a job title!

46: Commitment and courage

This is one of the most important chapters in this book. This is the message that I hope you remember the most out of all the ones given here. Everything in life takes commitment and courage; therefore, in order to proceed and progress into a better life, you have to learn how to have these two characteristics.

Everything in this life depends on your commitment and your courage. It takes commitment and courage to keep going when things are tough. It takes commitment and courage to get up from a downfall. It takes commitment and courage to move on from the things that have damaged us. It takes commitment and courage to forgive a person who has mistreated you. It takes commitment and courage to stand out from the crowd. It takes commitment and courage to follow your passion. It takes commitment and courage to avoid the discouragements of others. It takes commitment and courage to open your own business. It takes commitment and courage to try again. It takes commitment and courage to never give up.

Yes, I know, I have repeated "commitment and courage" many times in that last paragraph. I've done that purposely in order to really drill that inside of your head.

I want you to never forget how everything in this life requires your commitment and courage.

Do you want to start your own business, record music, or even write your own book? It takes your commitment to go after everything that is needed. It takes your commitment to do research about what is required. It takes your commitment to go after it, even if you have to keep a daily job to pay your bills. It takes your commitment to never give up on your dream. It also takes courage to avoid the negative things you might find along the way, or the negative feedback you might get from what you are offering. It takes courage to stand out from the crowd and do what you love despite what anybody says. It takes courage to keep going.

Nothing comes to you. You are the product of what you are committed to. You are as strong as your courage to never give up. You are it. Be committed. Be courageous. Once you learn that it takes YOU to be committed and courageous to do whatever you want, you will eventually start accomplishing anything you set your mind to.

47: The only thing stopping you

"It will come if you hold it close to your heart and firmly in your mind." ~ Daniel Chidiac

The only thing that is stopping you from achieving your full potential is you! That's right! You might have things that are holding you back, but the only thing stopping you from being who you want to be is you!

People love making excuses. Stop and look at the people you know or the people around you. Notice how most of them have something they want to do, but they make excuses for why they can't do it. That can either be being healthier or wealthier. It can be about learning another language or a new skill. Some make excuses for starting a new product or business. They make excuses for why they can't go to school or change jobs. They are always making excuses. I learned that no matter the circumstance you are in, you can always go after what you want, you just have to get up and start doing it.

I know many will disagree with me and say that sometimes there are things that hold us back. It can be that you don't have the proper documentation to go after something, the proper license, or even the money. That's understandable. However, when we consider that there are many things we can start to do now such as studying, planning, or even saving a couple dollars each week, you start to notice the many excuses we make to reach our full potential. Think about it. What do you want to be in life, what do you want to leave behind, and what goals do you want to accomplish it? Most of the things we want we can start to act now to get them. You want to be an engineer but can't afford to go to school now? You can start spending time studying the proper skills you need for it. You can walk into any library and pick any book to start learning today. This applies to each and everything we want out of our lives. The only thing you need to reach your full potential is you!

Stop making excuses, go after the things you want. There are many things that can be done in the process of waiting for the other things to get better. You don't have to wait until you attain something to start going after the things you want. Start today by imagining your life in the future. What is it that you want to have accomplished it? What is it that you want to learn? Where do you want to live? Once you figure that out, you can start acting on your goals today, even if it is little by little. The only thing stopping you from being you is yourself!

48: Tetris

"The key to enjoying the journey is being open to the unknown." – Kristine Carlson

The game of Tetris is very similar to the game of life. Ever been in a situation where you want something to happen a certain way but something else comes along and suddenly you must deal with it? We all have. Simply because it doesn't matter how much we plan our lives, somethings come along and changes our perspective. Sometimes that certain situation changes our lives completely, and other times it just adds a quick stop. Similar to Tetris. How many times were you playing Tetris and all you needed to clear a row was a straight line, but then a square came along and ruined your game? Sometimes that square may ruin your entire game, forcing you to start over. While other times, it might just be a quick stop and you will have to find ways to work around it.

Don't let that "square" stop you. Sometimes things happen to us that we feel so lost that we don't know what to do. Take a moment, analyze the "game," and make your next move. Life will throw us curve balls, forcing us to look at things differently. But it's during those moments that we grow the most.

I have been in situations in my life where I was so lost and confused about why such a thing would happen. But when I take a step back and look at the situation through a different perspective, I'm able to see that even the bad things that happen to me, or the bad things I have done, all happen to remind me of what I want for myself. Even when sometimes it seems like it is the worst thing ever, I try to remind myself of what's important and how the bad situation can provide me a great outcome.

As mentioned many times in this book, everything happens for a reason, and sometimes these reasons are unknown. However, when we are open to receive these unknown "shapes," life becomes fuller. Knowing this doesn't mean that you are not upset when something goes wrong, it means that you learn to accept it, and you deal with it. You learn to proceed with your life and progress into something new. Remember, life is like a game of Tetris, we must play around with the shapes that are given to us and never forget our ultimate goals!

49: Inspirations

What inspires you? What keeps you going? What makes you happy? We all need inspirations to get through our lives. When things are bad, we need something or someone to inspire us to keep going. When things are good, we need inspirations to make them even better. This chapter is dedicated to everything that inspires me.

Throughout this book, I have mentioned many people that I look up to, such as Richard and Kristine Carlson, Bob Proctor, and Prince EA. I want to take a moment to thank each person mentioned in this book as they have inspired me to write many of the things I talked about. These people "said" the right things to me in the right moments. Sometimes I would have something dangling in my mind, and somehow, I would read or listen to you guys, and you guys would solve an issue I had, help me understand a situation I was in, or simply inspired me to keep going. Richard Carlson, the author of the book, *Don't Sweat the Small Stuff*, brought light into my hard moments and inspired me to not worry so much about everything. Also, he has helped me solve the puzzle of what I wanted to become in my life. Bob Proctor's genius mind has helped me stay focus on what I wanted, and if I believed in it, I could attain it. Prince

EA's YouTube videos have made me look at life from a different perspective, and have inspired me to keep going after my dreams, even at times I wasn't so sure what I was doing. His video titled, *Everybody Dies, But Not Everybody Lives,* gave me the inspiration I needed to make this dream of publishing this book come to life. Along with the inspirations from these people mentioned here, and those mentioned throughout the book, I have learned to find inspirations in many other things that come into my life. As I mentioned, I find meaning in everything, such as movies and music. Sometimes that movie or that song can be completely inspiring, and other times it's just a scene or a verse. The point is that I find inspirations in many different things and many different people. We must learn to seek inspirations and be an inspiration. Seeking inspirations is allowing ourselves to feel inspired. It's allowing ourselves to be vulnerable to a message. It's allowing ourselves to gain knowledge at all times from those above us, or below us. The sense of finding inspirations in small or big things makes us happy. It helps us stay motivated, and makes us want to do our very best in any situation.

The point of the chapter is not to just praise those that have inspired me, but it's to show you the power of inspirations. Some of these people mentioned here, or the things that were quoted in this book, have inspired me to write, have inspired me to live better, have inspired me to worry less, and have inspired me to be happier. Allow yourself to connect to the messages of the world. Seek inspirations and be an inspiration to others!

50: To proceed and progress

As we come to the end of this book, I can't describe how proud I am of myself for doing this. It surely does take commitment and courage to follow your dreams. I hope this book has inspired you to live a better life as it did for me writing it. There were many different lessons in this book, but the main focus on all of them was the same: to learn to *proceed and progress* into a better life . . . a happier life.

It doesn't matter your job title, your age, your health, or your wealth, we are all learning to proceed and progress in our lives. To proceed and progress is about learning that life has its ups and downs. It is about learning that feelings, emotions, and situations can change. It is about learning to keep moving forward when things get tough. And most importantly, it is about learning how to live happier! We proceed with our lives when learning to deal with downfalls. We progress into new roles and adventures. We adapt to challenges and changes, and so on.

In order to actually proceed and progress into a better life, we must learn the strategies that were listed in this book. We must learn that everything happens for a reason, and even if what happened was bad, we can learn something from it. We must learn that a page can be flipped, and be positive that something good can come. We must learn to accept our mistakes and gain knowledge from them. We must learn to follow our dreams even when there are others that may doubt us. We must learn to have empathy for others that don't think the way we do. We must learn that bad days are what make the good days more exciting. We must learn to be responsible adults with the heart of a loving kid. We must learn to enjoy being alone and listen to what our hearts are telling us. We must learn to not sweat the small stuff and stress less. We must learn that sometimes we will struggle, but we can't possibly know what tomorrow will bring us. We must learn to respect others' opinions while still believing in our own, as everybody is equal. We must learn to face our fears as they can ultimately lead us to amazing things. We must learn that we can always do what we set our minds to, even if sometimes things will come along and add some "traffic." We must learn happiness is a mood like any other, and that NOBODY is always happy. We must learn to live a life where we can leave a legacy behind. We must learn to do what we love. Most importantly, we must learn to proceed and progress!

Life is, in fact, a rollercoaster that will go up and down, but when we learn to enjoy the ride, we become happier people. We must keep pushing forward even when there might be a big mountain in front of us as we don't know what the uphill battle will bring along the way or what the end of the journey consists of. This is what *PROCEED PROGRESS* is all about: learning to live a better life . . . learning to live a happier life!

Thank you!

I want to thank you for taking the time to read this book. I hope my stories can help you be better than what you are already! I hope to have encouraged you to pursue your passions and be happier. The main goal of this book was to inspire people to be their very best and to add value to the world. I want to share this positivity and encouragement to as many people as I can; therefore, if you enjoyed this book, share it with as many people as you possibly can! Anybody can be a source of inspiration about something they are truly passionate about, and that is what I want to be to others. I want to spread positivity and empower people to be happier. That's my mission. Let's help people together! Feel free to write to me or post online how this book has made you feel! I look forward to reading your stories.

Thank you!

@ProceedProgressBook

#ProceedProgressBook

References

Achor, S. (2010). The Happiness Advantage. The Crown Publishing Group.

Achor, S. (2013). Before Happiness: The 5 Hidden Keys to Achieving Sucess, Spreading Happiness, and Sustaining Positive Change. The Crown Publishing Group.

Ben-Shahar, B. (2012). Choose the Life You Want: 101 Ways to Create Your Own Road to Happiness. The Experiment.

Byrne, R. (2006). The Secret. New York: Atria Books.

Carlson, R. (1997). Don't Sweat the Small Stuff - and it's all small stuff. Simple ways to keep the little things from taking over your life. New York: Hyperion.

Carlson, R., & Carlson, K. (2000). Don't Sweat the Small Stuff - in Love. Hachette Books.

Carrey, J. (2014). Full Speech: Jim Carrey's Commencement Address at the 2014 MUM Graduation. Retrieved from

Maharishi University of Management: https://www.youtube.com/watch?v=V8 0-gPkpH6M&t=57s

Clements, R., & Musker, J. (Directors). (1992). Alladin [Motion Picture].

Muccino, G. (Director). (2006). The Pursuit of Happyness [Motion Picture].

Olson, A. (2014). Psychosis and the Eriksonian Stages. Retrieved from Psychology Today: https://www.psychologytoday.com/blog /theory-and- psychopathology/201405/psychosis- and-the-eriksonian-stages

Proctor, B. (2015). The ABCs of Sucess: The Essential Principles from America's Greatest Prosperity Teacher. Penguin Publishing Group.

Proctor, B. (2015). What is the Law of Vibration? Retrieved from Proctor Gallagher Institute: https://www.youtube.com/watch?v=P8 vHa8zD7jY

Smith, W. (2016). Inspiring Interview of Will Smith on December 2016 - How to Face Fear. Retrieved from Quiknugs TV: https://www.youtube.com/watch?v=IR pi1NwHOac&t=558s

Williams, R. (2016). EVERYBODY DIES, BUT NOT EVERYBODY LIVES.

Retrieved from Prince EA:
https://www.youtube.com/watch?v=ja-n5qUNRi8

Williams, R. (2016). Why You Shouldn't End
Your Relationship. Retrieved from
Prince EA:
https://www.youtube.com/watch?v=N_WkPAzj0xQ

90926063R00083

Made in the USA
Columbia, SC
13 March 2018